50 Homemade Cooking Recipes for Home

By: Kelly Johnson

Table of Contents

- Classic Meatloaf
- Creamy Chicken Alfredo
- Beef Tacos
- Homemade Lasagna
- Spaghetti Carbonara
- Chicken Curry
- Vegetable Stir-Fry
- Baked Ziti
- Stuffed Bell Peppers
- Quiche Lorraine
- Grilled Cheese Sandwich
- Chicken Fajitas
- Beef Stroganoff
- Shrimp Scampi
- Chili con Carne
- Clam Chowder
- Eggplant Parmesan
- Pulled Pork Sandwiches
- Ratatouille
- Mushroom Risotto
- Chicken Pot Pie
- Garlic Butter Steak
- Teriyaki Chicken
- Roasted Vegetable Medley
- Creamy Tomato Soup
- Pad Thai
- Shrimp Tacos
- Beef and Broccoli
- Spinach and Feta Stuffed Chicken
- BBQ Ribs
- Lemon Herb Grilled Chicken
- Stuffed Cabbage Rolls
- Sweet and Sour Pork
- Chicken Parmesan
- Mushroom and Spinach Frittata

- Beef Enchiladas
- Cauliflower Mac and Cheese
- French Onion Soup
- Jambalaya
- Baked Salmon with Dill
- Sloppy Joes
- Chicken and Dumplings
- Vegan Chili
- Butternut Squash Soup
- Fish Tacos
- Homemade Pizza
- Bangers and Mash
- Chicken Shawarma
- Falafel Wraps
- Chocolate Chip Cookies

Classic Meatloaf

Ingredients:

- 1 ½ lbs ground beef
- 1 cup breadcrumbs
- 1 onion, chopped
- 2 cloves garlic, minced
- 2 eggs
- 1 cup milk
- 1/4 cup ketchup (plus more for topping)
- 1 teaspoon Worcestershire sauce
- Salt and pepper (to taste)

Instructions:

1. **Preheat Oven**: Preheat the oven to 350°F (175°C).
2. **Mix Ingredients**: In a large bowl, combine ground beef, breadcrumbs, onion, garlic, eggs, milk, ketchup, Worcestershire sauce, salt, and pepper. Mix until well combined.
3. **Shape and Bake**: Shape the mixture into a loaf and place in a greased baking dish. Spread additional ketchup on top if desired.
4. **Bake**: Bake for 1 hour or until cooked through. Let rest for 10 minutes before slicing.

Creamy Chicken Alfredo

Ingredients:

- 12 oz fettuccine pasta
- 2 cups cooked chicken, diced
- 1 cup heavy cream
- 1/2 cup Parmesan cheese, grated
- 2 tablespoons butter
- 2 cloves garlic, minced
- Salt and pepper (to taste)
- Parsley (for garnish)

Instructions:

1. **Cook Pasta**: Cook fettuccine according to package instructions; drain.
2. **Make Sauce**: In a large skillet, melt butter over medium heat. Add garlic and sauté for 1 minute. Pour in heavy cream and simmer for 2-3 minutes. Stir in Parmesan cheese until melted. Season with salt and pepper.
3. **Combine**: Add cooked pasta and chicken to the sauce, tossing to combine.
4. **Serve**: Garnish with parsley and serve hot.

Beef Tacos

Ingredients:

- 1 lb ground beef
- 1 packet taco seasoning
- 1 cup water
- Taco shells or tortillas
- Toppings: shredded lettuce, diced tomatoes, cheese, sour cream, salsa

Instructions:

1. **Cook Beef**: In a skillet, cook ground beef over medium heat until browned. Drain excess fat.
2. **Season**: Stir in taco seasoning and water. Simmer for 5 minutes.
3. **Serve**: Fill taco shells or tortillas with the beef mixture and top with your favorite toppings.

Homemade Lasagna

Ingredients:

- 9 lasagna noodles
- 1 lb ground beef or Italian sausage
- 2 cups ricotta cheese
- 2 cups marinara sauce
- 2 cups mozzarella cheese, shredded
- 1/2 cup Parmesan cheese, grated
- 1 egg
- 1 teaspoon Italian seasoning
- Salt and pepper (to taste)

Instructions:

1. **Preheat Oven**: Preheat the oven to 375°F (190°C).
2. **Cook Noodles**: Boil lasagna noodles according to package instructions; drain.
3. **Brown Meat**: In a skillet, cook ground meat until browned. Drain fat and mix with marinara sauce.
4. **Mix Ricotta**: In a bowl, combine ricotta cheese, egg, Italian seasoning, salt, and pepper.
5. **Layer Ingredients**: In a greased baking dish, layer noodles, ricotta mixture, meat sauce, and mozzarella. Repeat layers, ending with mozzarella and Parmesan on top.
6. **Bake**: Cover with foil and bake for 30 minutes. Remove foil and bake for an additional 15-20 minutes until golden.

Spaghetti Carbonara

Ingredients:

- 12 oz spaghetti
- 4 oz pancetta or bacon, diced
- 2 eggs
- 1 cup Parmesan cheese, grated
- 2 cloves garlic, minced
- Salt and pepper (to taste)
- Parsley (for garnish)

Instructions:

1. **Cook Pasta**: Cook spaghetti according to package instructions; reserve 1 cup of pasta water before draining.
2. **Cook Pancetta**: In a skillet, cook pancetta over medium heat until crispy. Add garlic and sauté for 1 minute.
3. **Mix Eggs and Cheese**: In a bowl, whisk together eggs and Parmesan cheese. Season with salt and pepper.
4. **Combine**: Add hot pasta to the skillet with pancetta. Remove from heat and quickly stir in egg mixture, adding reserved pasta water as needed to create a creamy sauce.
5. **Serve**: Garnish with parsley and additional Parmesan.

Chicken Curry

Ingredients:

- 1 lb chicken, diced
- 1 onion, chopped
- 2 cloves garlic, minced
- 1 tablespoon ginger, minced
- 2 tablespoons curry powder
- 1 can (14 oz) coconut milk
- 1 cup chicken broth
- 2 cups mixed vegetables (peas, carrots, bell peppers)
- Salt and pepper (to taste)
- Rice (for serving)

Instructions:

1. **Sauté Vegetables**: In a large pot, sauté onion, garlic, and ginger until soft. Stir in curry powder.
2. **Add Chicken**: Add chicken and cook until browned. Pour in coconut milk and chicken broth; bring to a simmer.
3. **Add Vegetables**: Stir in mixed vegetables and simmer for 15-20 minutes until chicken is cooked through. Season with salt and pepper.
4. **Serve**: Serve hot over rice.

Vegetable Stir-Fry

Ingredients:

- 2 cups mixed vegetables (broccoli, bell peppers, carrots, snap peas)
- 2 tablespoons soy sauce
- 1 tablespoon sesame oil
- 2 cloves garlic, minced
- 1 tablespoon ginger, minced
- Cooked rice or noodles (for serving)

Instructions:

1. **Heat Oil**: In a large skillet or wok, heat sesame oil over medium-high heat.
2. **Sauté Garlic and Ginger**: Add garlic and ginger; sauté for 1 minute.
3. **Add Vegetables**: Stir in mixed vegetables and cook for 5-7 minutes until tender-crisp.
4. **Add Sauce**: Pour in soy sauce and stir to coat. Cook for an additional 1-2 minutes.
5. **Serve**: Serve hot over rice or noodles.

Baked Ziti

Ingredients:

- 12 oz ziti pasta
- 1 lb ground beef or Italian sausage
- 2 cups marinara sauce
- 2 cups ricotta cheese
- 2 cups mozzarella cheese, shredded
- 1/2 cup Parmesan cheese, grated
- 1 teaspoon Italian seasoning
- Salt and pepper (to taste)

Instructions:

1. **Preheat Oven**: Preheat the oven to 375°F (190°C).
2. **Cook Pasta**: Boil ziti according to package instructions; drain.
3. **Brown Meat**: In a skillet, cook ground meat until browned. Drain fat and stir in marinara sauce.
4. **Combine**: In a large bowl, mix cooked pasta, ricotta cheese, Italian seasoning, and meat sauce.
5. **Transfer to Dish**: Pour into a greased baking dish and top with mozzarella and Parmesan cheese.
6. **Bake**: Bake for 25-30 minutes until cheese is melted and bubbly.

Enjoy these delicious meals!

Stuffed Bell Peppers

Ingredients:

- 4 bell peppers (any color)
- 1 lb ground beef or turkey
- 1 cup cooked rice
- 1 can (15 oz) diced tomatoes
- 1 onion, chopped
- 1 teaspoon Italian seasoning
- Salt and pepper (to taste)
- 1 cup shredded cheese (cheddar or mozzarella)

Instructions:

1. **Preheat Oven**: Preheat the oven to 375°F (190°C).
2. **Prepare Peppers**: Cut the tops off the bell peppers and remove seeds. Place in a baking dish.
3. **Cook Filling**: In a skillet, sauté onion until soft. Add ground meat, cooking until browned. Stir in cooked rice, diced tomatoes, Italian seasoning, salt, and pepper.
4. **Stuff Peppers**: Fill each pepper with the meat mixture. Top with shredded cheese.
5. **Bake**: Bake for 25-30 minutes until peppers are tender.

Quiche Lorraine

Ingredients:

- 1 pie crust (store-bought or homemade)
- 6 slices bacon, cooked and crumbled
- 1 cup shredded Swiss cheese
- 4 large eggs
- 1 cup heavy cream
- Salt and pepper (to taste)
- 1/4 teaspoon nutmeg (optional)

Instructions:

1. **Preheat Oven**: Preheat the oven to 375°F (190°C).
2. **Prepare Crust**: Fit the pie crust into a pie dish and prick the bottom with a fork.
3. **Combine Ingredients**: In a bowl, whisk together eggs, heavy cream, salt, pepper, and nutmeg. Stir in bacon and Swiss cheese.
4. **Pour Filling**: Pour the mixture into the pie crust.
5. **Bake**: Bake for 30-35 minutes until set and golden. Let cool slightly before slicing.

Grilled Cheese Sandwich

Ingredients:

- 4 slices of bread (your choice)
- 4 slices of cheese (cheddar, American, or your preference)
- 2 tablespoons butter

Instructions:

1. **Heat Pan**: Heat a skillet over medium heat.
2. **Assemble Sandwich**: Butter one side of each slice of bread. Place cheese between two slices, buttered sides out.
3. **Cook**: Place the sandwich in the skillet and cook for 3-4 minutes per side until golden brown and cheese is melted.
4. **Serve**: Slice and serve hot.

Chicken Fajitas

Ingredients:

- 1 lb chicken breast, sliced
- 1 bell pepper, sliced
- 1 onion, sliced
- 2 tablespoons fajita seasoning
- 2 tablespoons olive oil
- Tortillas (for serving)
- Toppings: sour cream, salsa, guacamole

Instructions:

1. **Heat Oil**: In a skillet, heat olive oil over medium-high heat.
2. **Cook Chicken**: Add sliced chicken and cook until browned. Stir in bell pepper, onion, and fajita seasoning. Cook until vegetables are tender.
3. **Serve**: Serve in warm tortillas with desired toppings.

Beef Stroganoff

Ingredients:

- 1 lb beef sirloin, sliced
- 1 onion, chopped
- 2 cups mushrooms, sliced
- 2 cups beef broth
- 1 cup sour cream
- 2 tablespoons flour
- 2 tablespoons olive oil
- Salt and pepper (to taste)
- Egg noodles (for serving)

Instructions:

1. **Cook Beef**: In a skillet, heat olive oil over medium-high heat. Add beef and cook until browned. Remove and set aside.
2. **Sauté Vegetables**: In the same skillet, sauté onion and mushrooms until soft.
3. **Make Sauce**: Stir in flour and cook for 1 minute. Add beef broth and bring to a simmer. Return beef to the skillet.
4. **Add Sour Cream**: Remove from heat and stir in sour cream. Season with salt and pepper.
5. **Serve**: Serve over cooked egg noodles.

Shrimp Scampi

Ingredients:

- 1 lb shrimp, peeled and deveined
- 4 cloves garlic, minced
- 1/4 cup butter
- 1/4 cup white wine
- 1 lemon (juiced)
- 1/4 teaspoon red pepper flakes
- Salt and pepper (to taste)
- Fresh parsley (for garnish)
- Linguine or spaghetti (for serving)

Instructions:

1. **Cook Pasta**: Cook linguine or spaghetti according to package instructions; drain.
2. **Sauté Shrimp**: In a skillet, melt butter over medium heat. Add garlic and red pepper flakes; sauté for 1 minute. Add shrimp and cook until pink.
3. **Add Sauce**: Stir in white wine and lemon juice; simmer for a few minutes.
4. **Combine**: Toss cooked pasta with the shrimp mixture. Garnish with parsley and serve.

Chili con Carne

Ingredients:

- 1 lb ground beef
- 1 onion, chopped
- 2 cloves garlic, minced
- 1 can (15 oz) kidney beans, drained
- 1 can (15 oz) diced tomatoes
- 2 tablespoons chili powder
- 1 teaspoon cumin
- Salt and pepper (to taste)

Instructions:

1. **Cook Beef**: In a large pot, cook ground beef over medium heat until browned. Drain excess fat.
2. **Sauté Vegetables**: Add onion and garlic; sauté until soft.
3. **Add Ingredients**: Stir in kidney beans, diced tomatoes, chili powder, cumin, salt, and pepper.
4. **Simmer**: Bring to a simmer and cook for 20-30 minutes. Serve hot.

Clam Chowder

Ingredients:

- 4 slices bacon, chopped
- 1 onion, chopped
- 2 cups potatoes, diced
- 2 cups clam juice
- 1 cup heavy cream
- 1 can (15 oz) clams, drained
- 1 teaspoon thyme
- Salt and pepper (to taste)

Instructions:

1. **Cook Bacon**: In a large pot, cook bacon over medium heat until crispy. Remove and set aside.
2. **Sauté Onion**: In the bacon fat, sauté onion until soft. Add potatoes and clam juice; bring to a boil.
3. **Simmer**: Reduce heat and simmer until potatoes are tender (about 15 minutes).
4. **Add Clams and Cream**: Stir in heavy cream, clams, thyme, salt, and pepper. Heat through.
5. **Serve**: Garnish with crispy bacon before serving.

Enjoy these comforting and delicious dishes!

Eggplant Parmesan

Ingredients:

- 2 medium eggplants, sliced
- 2 cups marinara sauce
- 2 cups mozzarella cheese, shredded
- 1 cup Parmesan cheese, grated
- 1 cup breadcrumbs
- 2 eggs, beaten
- Olive oil (for frying)
- Salt and pepper (to taste)
- Fresh basil (for garnish)

Instructions:

1. **Preheat Oven**: Preheat the oven to 375°F (190°C).
2. **Prepare Eggplant**: Sprinkle eggplant slices with salt and let sit for 30 minutes to draw out moisture. Rinse and pat dry.
3. **Bread Eggplant**: Dip eggplant slices in beaten eggs, then coat with breadcrumbs.
4. **Fry Eggplant**: In a skillet, heat olive oil over medium heat. Fry eggplant slices until golden brown. Drain on paper towels.
5. **Assemble**: In a baking dish, layer marinara sauce, eggplant, mozzarella, and Parmesan. Repeat layers, finishing with cheese on top.
6. **Bake**: Bake for 25-30 minutes until bubbly and golden. Garnish with fresh basil before serving.

Pulled Pork Sandwiches

Ingredients:

- 3 lbs pork shoulder
- 1 cup barbecue sauce
- 1 onion, sliced
- 1 tablespoon garlic powder
- 1 tablespoon smoked paprika
- Salt and pepper (to taste)
- Burger buns (for serving)
- Coleslaw (optional, for topping)

Instructions:

1. **Slow Cook Pork**: Season pork shoulder with garlic powder, smoked paprika, salt, and pepper. Place in a slow cooker with sliced onion and cook on low for 8 hours, or until tender.
2. **Shred Pork**: Remove pork from the slow cooker and shred with two forks. Mix with barbecue sauce.
3. **Serve**: Pile shredded pork onto burger buns and top with coleslaw if desired.

Ratatouille

Ingredients:

- 1 eggplant, diced
- 2 zucchini, sliced
- 1 bell pepper, diced
- 1 onion, chopped
- 2 cups diced tomatoes (canned or fresh)
- 2 cloves garlic, minced
- 2 tablespoons olive oil
- 1 teaspoon thyme
- Salt and pepper (to taste)

Instructions:

1. **Sauté Vegetables**: In a large pot, heat olive oil over medium heat. Add onion and garlic; sauté until soft.
2. **Add Vegetables**: Stir in eggplant, zucchini, and bell pepper. Cook for about 5 minutes.
3. **Add Tomatoes and Seasoning**: Add diced tomatoes, thyme, salt, and pepper. Simmer for 20-30 minutes until vegetables are tender.
4. **Serve**: Enjoy warm as a side or main dish.

Mushroom Risotto

Ingredients:

- 1 cup Arborio rice
- 4 cups vegetable or chicken broth (warmed)
- 1 cup mushrooms, sliced
- 1 onion, chopped
- 2 cloves garlic, minced
- 1/2 cup white wine (optional)
- 1/2 cup Parmesan cheese, grated
- 2 tablespoons butter
- Salt and pepper (to taste)
- Fresh parsley (for garnish)

Instructions:

1. **Sauté Aromatics**: In a large pan, melt butter over medium heat. Add onion and garlic; sauté until translucent.
2. **Cook Mushrooms**: Add mushrooms and cook until softened.
3. **Toast Rice**: Stir in Arborio rice and cook for 1-2 minutes until lightly toasted.
4. **Add Wine**: Pour in white wine and stir until absorbed.
5. **Add Broth**: Gradually add warmed broth, one ladle at a time, stirring frequently until absorbed before adding more. Continue until rice is creamy and al dente (about 20-25 minutes).
6. **Finish Risotto**: Stir in Parmesan cheese, salt, and pepper. Garnish with fresh parsley before serving.

Chicken Pot Pie

Ingredients:

- 2 cups cooked chicken, shredded
- 1 cup frozen mixed vegetables
- 1/3 cup butter
- 1/3 cup flour
- 1 ½ cups chicken broth
- 1 cup milk
- 1 teaspoon thyme
- Salt and pepper (to taste)
- 1 pie crust (top and bottom)

Instructions:

1. **Preheat Oven**: Preheat the oven to 425°F (220°C).
2. **Make Filling**: In a saucepan, melt butter over medium heat. Stir in flour and cook for 1 minute. Gradually add chicken broth and milk, whisking until thickened. Stir in chicken, vegetables, thyme, salt, and pepper.
3. **Assemble Pie**: Pour filling into a pie crust-lined dish. Cover with the top crust, sealing edges and cutting slits for steam to escape.
4. **Bake**: Bake for 30-35 minutes until golden brown. Let cool for a few minutes before serving.

Garlic Butter Steak

Ingredients:

- 1 lb steak (ribeye, sirloin, or your choice)
- 4 tablespoons butter
- 4 cloves garlic, minced
- 1 teaspoon rosemary (fresh or dried)
- Salt and pepper (to taste)

Instructions:

1. **Season Steak**: Season steak with salt and pepper on both sides.
2. **Cook Steak**: In a skillet, heat 2 tablespoons of butter over medium-high heat. Add the steak and cook to your desired doneness (about 4-5 minutes per side for medium).
3. **Add Garlic Butter**: In the last minute of cooking, add remaining butter, garlic, and rosemary. Baste the steak with the melted garlic butter.
4. **Rest and Serve**: Remove from heat and let rest for 5 minutes before slicing.

Teriyaki Chicken

Ingredients:

- 1 lb chicken breast, diced
- 1/2 cup soy sauce
- 1/4 cup brown sugar
- 2 tablespoons rice vinegar
- 1 tablespoon sesame oil
- 2 cloves garlic, minced
- Green onions (for garnish)
- Cooked rice (for serving)

Instructions:

1. **Make Marinade**: In a bowl, mix soy sauce, brown sugar, rice vinegar, sesame oil, and garlic.
2. **Marinate Chicken**: Add diced chicken to the marinade and let sit for at least 30 minutes.
3. **Cook Chicken**: In a skillet over medium-high heat, cook marinated chicken until fully cooked (about 7-10 minutes).
4. **Serve**: Serve over cooked rice and garnish with sliced green onions.

Roasted Vegetable Medley

Ingredients:

- 2 cups mixed vegetables (carrots, zucchini, bell peppers, broccoli)
- 3 tablespoons olive oil
- 1 teaspoon Italian seasoning
- Salt and pepper (to taste)

Instructions:

1. **Preheat Oven**: Preheat the oven to 425°F (220°C).
2. **Prepare Vegetables**: Chop vegetables into uniform pieces. In a bowl, toss with olive oil, Italian seasoning, salt, and pepper.
3. **Roast**: Spread vegetables on a baking sheet in a single layer. Roast for 20-25 minutes until tender and slightly caramelized, stirring halfway through.
4. **Serve**: Enjoy warm as a side dish.

Enjoy these hearty and delicious meals!

Creamy Tomato Soup

Ingredients:

- 2 tablespoons olive oil
- 1 onion, chopped
- 2 cloves garlic, minced
- 2 cans (14 oz each) diced tomatoes
- 1 cup vegetable or chicken broth
- 1 teaspoon sugar
- Salt and pepper (to taste)
- 1/2 cup heavy cream
- Fresh basil (for garnish)

Instructions:

1. **Sauté Aromatics**: In a pot, heat olive oil over medium heat. Add onion and garlic; sauté until soft.
2. **Add Tomatoes**: Stir in diced tomatoes, broth, sugar, salt, and pepper. Bring to a simmer and cook for 15 minutes.
3. **Blend**: Use an immersion blender (or transfer to a blender) to puree the soup until smooth.
4. **Add Cream**: Stir in heavy cream and heat through. Garnish with fresh basil before serving.

Pad Thai

Ingredients:

- 8 oz rice noodles
- 2 tablespoons vegetable oil
- 1 egg, beaten
- 1 cup cooked shrimp or chicken
- 2 cups bean sprouts
- 2 green onions, chopped
- 1/4 cup peanuts, chopped
- 3 tablespoons fish sauce
- 2 tablespoons tamarind paste
- 1 tablespoon sugar
- Lime wedges (for serving)

Instructions:

1. **Cook Noodles**: Soak rice noodles in hot water until softened, about 10 minutes. Drain and set aside.
2. **Stir-Fry**: In a large skillet, heat oil over medium-high heat. Add beaten egg and scramble until cooked. Add shrimp or chicken, bean sprouts, and green onions; stir-fry for a few minutes.
3. **Add Noodles**: Add drained noodles, fish sauce, tamarind paste, and sugar. Toss everything together until well combined.
4. **Serve**: Top with chopped peanuts and lime wedges.

Shrimp Tacos

Ingredients:

- 1 lb shrimp, peeled and deveined
- 2 tablespoons olive oil
- 1 teaspoon chili powder
- 1 teaspoon cumin
- Salt and pepper (to taste)
- 8 small corn or flour tortillas
- Cabbage slaw (for topping)
- Avocado, sliced (for topping)
- Lime wedges (for serving)

Instructions:

1. **Season Shrimp**: In a bowl, toss shrimp with olive oil, chili powder, cumin, salt, and pepper.
2. **Cook Shrimp**: In a skillet, cook shrimp over medium heat for 2-3 minutes on each side until pink and cooked through.
3. **Assemble Tacos**: Warm tortillas and fill each with shrimp, cabbage slaw, and avocado slices. Serve with lime wedges.

Beef and Broccoli

Ingredients:

- 1 lb beef (flank or sirloin), sliced thinly
- 2 cups broccoli florets
- 3 tablespoons soy sauce
- 2 tablespoons oyster sauce
- 1 tablespoon cornstarch
- 2 tablespoons vegetable oil
- 2 cloves garlic, minced
- Cooked rice (for serving)

Instructions:

1. **Marinate Beef**: In a bowl, combine beef, soy sauce, oyster sauce, and cornstarch. Let marinate for 15 minutes.
2. **Cook Beef**: In a skillet, heat vegetable oil over medium-high heat. Add beef and cook until browned. Remove and set aside.
3. **Stir-Fry Broccoli**: In the same skillet, add broccoli and a splash of water. Cover and steam for 2-3 minutes until bright green and tender.
4. **Combine**: Add garlic and cooked beef back to the skillet. Stir-fry together for 2 minutes. Serve over cooked rice.

Spinach and Feta Stuffed Chicken

Ingredients:

- 4 chicken breasts
- 1 cup fresh spinach, chopped
- 1/2 cup feta cheese, crumbled
- 2 cloves garlic, minced
- 1 teaspoon dried oregano
- Salt and pepper (to taste)
- Olive oil (for drizzling)

Instructions:

1. **Preheat Oven**: Preheat the oven to 375°F (190°C).
2. **Prepare Filling**: In a bowl, mix spinach, feta, garlic, oregano, salt, and pepper.
3. **Stuff Chicken**: Cut a pocket in each chicken breast and fill with the spinach mixture. Secure with toothpicks if needed.
4. **Bake**: Place chicken in a baking dish, drizzle with olive oil, and bake for 25-30 minutes until cooked through.

BBQ Ribs

Ingredients:

- 2 racks of baby back ribs
- 1 cup BBQ sauce
- 2 tablespoons brown sugar
- 1 tablespoon smoked paprika
- Salt and pepper (to taste)

Instructions:

1. **Preheat Oven**: Preheat the oven to 300°F (150°C).
2. **Prepare Ribs**: Remove the silver skin from the ribs. Season with salt, pepper, brown sugar, and smoked paprika.
3. **Bake**: Place ribs on a baking sheet and cover with foil. Bake for 2.5 to 3 hours until tender.
4. **Glaze with BBQ**: Remove foil, brush with BBQ sauce, and bake for an additional 30 minutes. Serve hot.

Lemon Herb Grilled Chicken

Ingredients:

- 4 chicken breasts
- 1/4 cup olive oil
- 2 lemons (juiced and zested)
- 2 tablespoons fresh herbs (parsley, thyme, or rosemary)
- 3 cloves garlic, minced
- Salt and pepper (to taste)

Instructions:

1. **Marinate Chicken**: In a bowl, whisk together olive oil, lemon juice, lemon zest, herbs, garlic, salt, and pepper. Add chicken and marinate for at least 30 minutes.
2. **Preheat Grill**: Preheat the grill to medium-high heat.
3. **Grill Chicken**: Grill chicken for 6-7 minutes on each side until cooked through. Let rest for a few minutes before slicing.

Stuffed Cabbage Rolls

Ingredients:

- 1 large head of cabbage
- 1 lb ground beef or turkey
- 1 cup cooked rice
- 1 onion, chopped
- 1 can (15 oz) tomato sauce
- 1 teaspoon Italian seasoning
- Salt and pepper (to taste)

Instructions:

1. **Preheat Oven**: Preheat the oven to 350°F (175°C).
2. **Prepare Cabbage**: Bring a large pot of water to a boil. Carefully remove cabbage leaves and blanch for 2 minutes. Set aside.
3. **Make Filling**: In a bowl, mix ground meat, cooked rice, onion, tomato sauce, Italian seasoning, salt, and pepper.
4. **Stuff Rolls**: Place a spoonful of filling on each cabbage leaf and roll tightly. Place seam-side down in a baking dish.
5. **Bake**: Pour additional tomato sauce over rolls and cover. Bake for 45 minutes until cooked through.

Enjoy these delicious and comforting meals!

Sweet and Sour Pork

Ingredients:

- 1 lb pork tenderloin, diced
- 1 cup bell peppers, chopped
- 1 cup pineapple chunks (fresh or canned)
- 1 onion, chopped
- 2 cloves garlic, minced
- 1/2 cup sugar
- 1/2 cup vinegar
- 1/2 cup ketchup
- 1 tablespoon soy sauce
- Salt and pepper (to taste)
- Cooked rice (for serving)

Instructions:

1. **Cook Pork**: In a skillet, brown the pork over medium heat. Remove and set aside.
2. **Sauté Vegetables**: In the same skillet, add onion, garlic, and bell peppers. Sauté until softened.
3. **Make Sauce**: In a bowl, mix sugar, vinegar, ketchup, soy sauce, salt, and pepper. Pour over the vegetables.
4. **Combine**: Add the pork and pineapple to the skillet. Simmer for 10-15 minutes until heated through. Serve over rice.

Chicken Parmesan

Ingredients:

- 4 chicken breasts
- 1 cup breadcrumbs
- 1/2 cup Parmesan cheese, grated
- 1 cup marinara sauce
- 1 cup mozzarella cheese, shredded
- 2 eggs, beaten
- Olive oil (for frying)
- Fresh basil (for garnish)

Instructions:

1. **Preheat Oven**: Preheat the oven to 375°F (190°C).
2. **Bread Chicken**: Dip chicken in eggs, then coat with a mixture of breadcrumbs and Parmesan cheese.
3. **Fry Chicken**: In a skillet, heat olive oil over medium heat. Fry chicken until golden brown on both sides.
4. **Assemble**: Place chicken in a baking dish, top with marinara and mozzarella cheese. Bake for 20-25 minutes until cheese is bubbly. Garnish with basil before serving.

Mushroom and Spinach Frittata

Ingredients:

- 6 eggs
- 1 cup mushrooms, sliced
- 2 cups fresh spinach
- 1/2 cup cheese (cheddar or feta), crumbled
- 1 onion, chopped
- 2 tablespoons olive oil
- Salt and pepper (to taste)

Instructions:

1. **Preheat Oven**: Preheat the oven to 375°F (190°C).
2. **Sauté Vegetables**: In an oven-safe skillet, heat olive oil over medium heat. Add onion and mushrooms; sauté until softened. Stir in spinach until wilted.
3. **Whisk Eggs**: In a bowl, whisk together eggs, cheese, salt, and pepper. Pour over the vegetables in the skillet.
4. **Cook**: Cook on the stovetop for 2-3 minutes until edges set, then transfer to the oven. Bake for 15-20 minutes until fully set. Slice and serve warm.

Beef Enchiladas

Ingredients:

- 1 lb ground beef
- 1 can (10 oz) enchilada sauce
- 1 cup shredded cheese (cheddar or Monterey Jack)
- 8 corn tortillas
- 1 onion, chopped
- 1 teaspoon cumin
- Salt and pepper (to taste)

Instructions:

1. **Cook Beef**: In a skillet, cook ground beef and onion until browned. Stir in cumin, salt, and pepper.
2. **Prepare Tortillas**: Warm tortillas in a skillet or microwave to soften.
3. **Assemble Enchiladas**: Spread some enchilada sauce in a baking dish. Fill each tortilla with beef and cheese, roll up, and place seam-side down in the dish. Top with remaining sauce and cheese.
4. **Bake**: Bake at 350°F (175°C) for 20-25 minutes until cheese is melted and bubbly.

Cauliflower Mac and Cheese

Ingredients:

- 1 head of cauliflower, cut into florets
- 2 cups cheese (cheddar or your choice), shredded
- 1/2 cup milk
- 2 tablespoons butter
- 1/4 cup breadcrumbs
- Salt and pepper (to taste)

Instructions:

1. **Cook Cauliflower**: Boil cauliflower florets in salted water for 5-7 minutes until tender. Drain and set aside.
2. **Make Cheese Sauce**: In a saucepan, melt butter, then stir in milk and cheese until melted and smooth. Season with salt and pepper.
3. **Combine**: Mix cauliflower with cheese sauce. Pour into a baking dish, top with breadcrumbs.
4. **Bake**: Bake at 350°F (175°C) for 20-25 minutes until golden brown.

French Onion Soup

Ingredients:

- 4 large onions, thinly sliced
- 4 cups beef broth
- 2 tablespoons butter
- 1 tablespoon olive oil
- 1 teaspoon thyme
- Baguette slices
- 1 cup Gruyère cheese, grated

Instructions:

1. **Caramelize Onions**: In a large pot, melt butter and olive oil over medium heat. Add onions and cook, stirring frequently, for 30-40 minutes until caramelized.
2. **Add Broth**: Stir in beef broth and thyme. Simmer for 15 minutes.
3. **Toast Bread**: While soup simmers, toast baguette slices.
4. **Serve**: Ladle soup into bowls, top with toasted bread, and sprinkle cheese on top. Broil until cheese is bubbly.

Jambalaya

Ingredients:

- 1 lb sausage (Andouille or your choice), sliced
- 1 lb shrimp, peeled and deveined
- 1 bell pepper, chopped
- 1 onion, chopped
- 2 cups rice
- 4 cups chicken broth
- 1 can (14.5 oz) diced tomatoes
- 2 teaspoons Cajun seasoning
- Salt and pepper (to taste)

Instructions:

1. **Cook Sausage**: In a large pot, brown sausage over medium heat. Add onion and bell pepper; cook until softened.
2. **Add Rice**: Stir in rice, diced tomatoes, chicken broth, Cajun seasoning, salt, and pepper. Bring to a boil.
3. **Simmer**: Reduce heat, cover, and simmer for 20-25 minutes until rice is cooked. Add shrimp and cook until pink.
4. **Serve**: Fluff with a fork and serve warm.

Baked Salmon with Dill

Ingredients:

- 4 salmon fillets
- 2 tablespoons olive oil
- 2 tablespoons fresh dill (or 1 tablespoon dried)
- 1 lemon, sliced
- Salt and pepper (to taste)

Instructions:

1. **Preheat Oven**: Preheat the oven to 375°F (190°C).
2. **Prepare Salmon**: Place salmon fillets on a baking sheet lined with parchment paper. Drizzle with olive oil and sprinkle with dill, salt, and pepper. Top with lemon slices.
3. **Bake**: Bake for 15-20 minutes until salmon is cooked through and flakes easily with a fork. Serve warm.

Enjoy these flavorful and satisfying dishes!

Sloppy Joes

Ingredients:

- 1 lb ground beef or turkey
- 1 onion, chopped
- 1 bell pepper, chopped
- 1 cup ketchup
- 2 tablespoons brown sugar
- 1 tablespoon Worcestershire sauce
- 1 teaspoon mustard
- Salt and pepper (to taste)
- Burger buns (for serving)

Instructions:

1. **Cook Meat**: In a skillet, brown the ground meat over medium heat. Drain excess fat.
2. **Sauté Vegetables**: Add onion and bell pepper; cook until softened.
3. **Mix Sauce**: Stir in ketchup, brown sugar, Worcestershire sauce, mustard, salt, and pepper. Simmer for 10 minutes.
4. **Serve**: Spoon mixture onto burger buns and enjoy!

Chicken and Dumplings

Ingredients:

- 1 lb chicken breast, cooked and shredded
- 4 cups chicken broth
- 2 cups mixed vegetables (carrots, peas, corn)
- 2 cups flour
- 1 tablespoon baking powder
- 1/2 teaspoon salt
- 1 cup milk
- 1/4 cup butter, melted

Instructions:

1. **Simmer Chicken**: In a pot, bring chicken broth to a boil. Add shredded chicken and mixed vegetables.
2. **Make Dumplings**: In a bowl, combine flour, baking powder, and salt. Stir in milk and melted butter until just combined.
3. **Add Dumplings**: Drop spoonfuls of the dough into the boiling broth. Cover and simmer for 15-20 minutes until dumplings are cooked through.
4. **Serve**: Ladle into bowls and enjoy warm.

Vegan Chili

Ingredients:

- 1 can (15 oz) black beans, drained and rinsed
- 1 can (15 oz) kidney beans, drained and rinsed
- 1 can (15 oz) diced tomatoes
- 1 onion, chopped
- 1 bell pepper, chopped
- 2 cloves garlic, minced
- 2 tablespoons chili powder
- 1 teaspoon cumin
- Salt and pepper (to taste)

Instructions:

1. **Sauté Vegetables**: In a pot, heat a bit of oil over medium heat. Add onion, bell pepper, and garlic; cook until softened.
2. **Add Ingredients**: Stir in black beans, kidney beans, diced tomatoes, chili powder, cumin, salt, and pepper. Bring to a simmer.
3. **Cook**: Simmer for 20-30 minutes, stirring occasionally. Adjust seasoning if needed.
4. **Serve**: Enjoy with your favorite toppings!

Butternut Squash Soup

Ingredients:

- 1 medium butternut squash, peeled and cubed
- 1 onion, chopped
- 2 cloves garlic, minced
- 4 cups vegetable broth
- 1 teaspoon thyme
- Salt and pepper (to taste)
- Olive oil (for drizzling)

Instructions:

1. **Sauté Onions**: In a pot, heat olive oil over medium heat. Add onion and garlic; sauté until softened.
2. **Cook Squash**: Add butternut squash, vegetable broth, thyme, salt, and pepper. Bring to a boil.
3. **Simmer**: Reduce heat and simmer for 20-25 minutes until squash is tender.
4. **Blend**: Use an immersion blender to puree until smooth. Serve warm.

Fish Tacos

Ingredients:

- 1 lb white fish (like cod or tilapia)
- 1 tablespoon olive oil
- 1 teaspoon chili powder
- Salt and pepper (to taste)
- 8 small tortillas
- Cabbage slaw (for topping)
- Lime wedges (for serving)

Instructions:

1. **Season Fish**: Rub fish with olive oil, chili powder, salt, and pepper.
2. **Cook Fish**: In a skillet, cook fish over medium heat for about 3-4 minutes on each side until cooked through. Flake with a fork.
3. **Assemble Tacos**: Warm tortillas and fill with flaked fish and cabbage slaw. Serve with lime wedges.

Homemade Pizza

Ingredients:

- 1 pizza dough (store-bought or homemade)
- 1/2 cup pizza sauce
- 1 1/2 cups mozzarella cheese, shredded
- Toppings of choice (pepperoni, vegetables, etc.)
- Olive oil (for brushing)

Instructions:

1. **Preheat Oven**: Preheat the oven to 475°F (245°C).
2. **Prepare Dough**: Roll out the pizza dough on a floured surface to your desired thickness. Place on a baking sheet or pizza stone.
3. **Assemble Pizza**: Spread pizza sauce over the dough, sprinkle with mozzarella, and add desired toppings.
4. **Bake**: Brush edges with olive oil and bake for 12-15 minutes until cheese is bubbly and crust is golden.

Bangers and Mash

Ingredients:

- 6 sausages (pork or your choice)
- 2 lbs potatoes, peeled and cubed
- 1/2 cup milk
- 1/4 cup butter
- Salt and pepper (to taste)
- Onion gravy (optional)

Instructions:

1. **Cook Sausages**: In a skillet, cook sausages over medium heat until browned and cooked through.
2. **Boil Potatoes**: In a pot, boil potatoes until tender. Drain and return to pot.
3. **Mash**: Add milk, butter, salt, and pepper to potatoes. Mash until smooth and creamy.
4. **Serve**: Plate sausages with mashed potatoes and drizzle with onion gravy if desired.

Chicken Shawarma

Ingredients:

- 1 lb chicken thighs, sliced
- 2 tablespoons olive oil
- 2 teaspoons cumin
- 2 teaspoons paprika
- 1 teaspoon garlic powder
- Salt and pepper (to taste)
- Pita bread (for serving)
- Toppings: lettuce, tomatoes, cucumber, tahini sauce

Instructions:

1. **Marinate Chicken**: In a bowl, mix olive oil, cumin, paprika, garlic powder, salt, and pepper. Add chicken and marinate for at least 30 minutes.
2. **Cook Chicken**: In a skillet, cook chicken over medium heat until browned and cooked through.
3. **Assemble Wraps**: Fill pita bread with cooked chicken and your choice of toppings. Drizzle with tahini sauce and serve.

Enjoy these hearty and delicious dishes!

Falafel Wraps

Ingredients:

- 1 can (15 oz) chickpeas, drained and rinsed
- 1/4 cup onion, chopped
- 2 cloves garlic, minced
- 1/4 cup fresh parsley, chopped
- 1 teaspoon cumin
- 1 teaspoon coriander
- Salt and pepper (to taste)
- 1/4 cup flour
- Oil (for frying)
- Pita bread or wraps
- Toppings: lettuce, tomatoes, cucumber, tahini sauce

Instructions:

1. **Make Falafel Mixture**: In a food processor, combine chickpeas, onion, garlic, parsley, cumin, coriander, salt, and pepper. Pulse until coarse. Add flour and pulse until mixed.
2. **Form Patties**: Shape the mixture into small patties or balls.
3. **Fry Falafel**: Heat oil in a skillet over medium heat. Fry the falafel until golden brown, about 3-4 minutes per side. Drain on paper towels.
4. **Assemble Wraps**: Fill pita or wraps with falafel, lettuce, tomatoes, cucumber, and drizzle with tahini sauce. Roll up and enjoy!

Chocolate Chip Cookies

Ingredients:

- 1 cup butter, softened
- 3/4 cup brown sugar
- 3/4 cup granulated sugar
- 1 teaspoon vanilla extract
- 2 large eggs
- 2 1/4 cups all-purpose flour
- 1 teaspoon baking soda
- 1/2 teaspoon salt
- 2 cups chocolate chips

Instructions:

1. **Preheat Oven**: Preheat the oven to 375°F (190°C).
2. **Cream Butter and Sugars**: In a large bowl, cream together softened butter, brown sugar, granulated sugar, and vanilla until smooth.
3. **Add Eggs**: Beat in eggs one at a time until well combined.
4. **Mix Dry Ingredients**: In another bowl, whisk together flour, baking soda, and salt. Gradually add to the butter mixture. Stir in chocolate chips.
5. **Bake Cookies**: Drop rounded tablespoons of dough onto ungreased baking sheets. Bake for 9-11 minutes until golden. Let cool on sheets for a few minutes before transferring to wire racks.

Enjoy your falafel wraps and warm chocolate chip cookies!

www.ingramcontent.com/pod-product-compliance
Lightning Source LLC
LaVergne TN
LVHW061955070526
838199LV00060B/4124

9798330437115